FIELD GUIDES

BUTTERFLIES

Laura Lane

Abdo Reference

An Imprint of Abdo Publishing | abdobooks.com

CONTENTS

WHAT ARE BUTTERFLIES?

Insects first developed the ability to fly millions of years ago. Today, butterflies are some of the most beautiful and colorful insects on Earth. They live in diverse habitats, including tropical rain forests, the Arctic tundra, mountain slopes, grasslands, and more. Butterflies are found on every continent except Antarctica. They have four wings, and they live as caterpillars before transforming into adult butterflies.

WHAT ARE BUTTERFLIES LIKE?

Butterflies come in a wide range of sizes. The largest butterfly in the world is Queen Alexandra's birdwing. It lives in the rain forests of New Guinea. Its wingspan can grow to 12 inches (30 cm). The smallest butterfly in the world is the North American pygmy blue, which has a wingspan of less than 1 inch (2.5 cm). Butterflies are ectothermic, which means they depend on external sources to control their body temperatures. The best time for them to fly is when the air temperature is 82 to 100 degrees Fahrenheit (28 to 38°C). Butterflies' wings are covered in scales that help keep them warm. The scales can either reflect or absorb light, which gives the wings different colors.

Butterflies have some key features in common:

- Butterflies' bodies have three parts: a head, a thorax, and an abdomen.

- The body has a hard covering called an exoskeleton.

- The head has a pair of eyes, a pair of antennae, and mouth parts.

- The thorax has two pairs of wings and three pairs of legs attached to it.

- The upper wings on each side are called the forewings. The lower wings are called the hindwings and can have tails. The forewings tend to be bigger than the hindwings.

LIFE CYCLE AND ROLES

The life cycle of a butterfly has four stages:

- Egg

- Caterpillar

- Chrysalis

- Adult butterfly

Caterpillars look completely different from adult butterflies. However, both caterpillars and adult butterflies are herbivores, or plant eaters. Butterflies commonly eat flower nectar. They also pollinate flowering plants. Butterflies are food for predators such as spiders, birds, lizards, and small mammals.

HOW TO USE THIS BOOK

Tab shows the butterfly category.

BRUSH-FOOTED BUTTERFLIES

OWL BUTTERFLY (CALIGO MEMNON)

The owl butterfly is one of the largest butterflies in the world. It is also known as the giant owl or pale owl. These _____ patterns. Their forewings _____ borders. The hindwings are _____ are brown and gray. Each _____ looks like an owl eye. This _____ dusk.

The butterfly's common name appears here.

HOW TO SPOT

Size: Wingspan of 4.8 to 5.3 inches (12.2 to 13.5 cm)

Range: Central and South America

Habitat: Tropical rain forests

Diet: Rotting fruits and animal dung

How to Spot boxes give information about the butterfly's size, range, habitat, and diet.

FOOLING PREDATORS

When owl butterflies close their wings, predators see large eyespots. The eyespots confuse predators. They might bite the eyespots, thinking they've found the butterfly's _____ erflies can still fly away even if part of a

Sidebars provide additional information about the topic.

20

6

PAINTED LADY *(VANESSA CARDUI)*

The butterfly's scientific name appears here.

Painted ladies are the most widespread butterflies in the world and can be found on almost every continent. These butterflies have brown and orange forewings. Their black wingtips have white spots. The undersides of the hindwings have small spots near the edges. Painted ladies sometimes have a small area of blue coloring on each hindwing. These butterflies are able to travel great distances.

The paragraph gives information about the butterfly.

HOW TO SPOT

Size: Wi
2.9 inc
Range:
except
Antarcti
Habitat: Open a
such as meadows,
gardens, and vacant lots
Diet: Flower nectar,
especially from thistles

Images show the butterfly.

FUN FACT
The painted lady is a strong and fast flier. It can fly up to 620 miles (1,000 km) at a speed of 9 miles per hour (14 km/h).

Fun Facts give interesting information about the butterfly.

AFRICAN MAP BUTTERFLY
(CYRESTIS CAMILLUS)

African map butterflies have white wings with orange and brown lines. They also have black borders around their wings. Each hindwing has two blue spots. African map butterflies glide gracefully in circles close to the ground. They are usually spotted in groups of two or three. These butterflies rest on the ground with their wings outstretched. African map butterflies live in forests and often take shelter under leaves.

HOW TO SPOT

Size: Wingspan of 2.2 inches (5.6 cm)
Range: Africa, Mozambique, and Madagascar
Habitat: Forests
Diet: Flower nectar

AMERICAN PAINTED LADY
(VANESSA VIRGINIENSIS)

The American painted lady is a brown, yellow, and orange butterfly. Each forewing has a dark patch near the top with small, white spots. There are two large eyespots on the underside of each hindwing. Males perch on hilltops in the afternoon and sip water from damp soil and mud. Females fly low and lay tiny, green eggs on host plants.

HOW TO SPOT

Size: Wingspan of 1.8 to 2.6 inches (4.6 to 6.6 cm)

Range: United States, Mexico, Central America, Colombia, Canary Islands, Madeira, Hawaii, and the Galápagos Islands

Habitat: Meadows, parks, dunes, vacant lots, and forest edges

Diet: Nectar from flowers including asters, goldenrods, and marigolds; sap or rotting fruits

FUN FACT
The American painted lady is a strong flier. It can travel up to 100 miles (160 km) a day during migration.

ARCTIC FRITILLARY
(BOLORIA CHARICLEA)

The Arctic fritillary is an orange-brown butterfly with dark markings on its wings. Males fly along edges of valleys and bogs in search of females to mate with. Females lay single eggs on the leaves of host plants, including violets and blueberries.

HOW TO SPOT

Size: Wingspan of 1.3 to 1.5 inches (3.3 to 3.8 cm)
Range: North America and Northern Asia
Habitat: Alpine meadows, tundras, and taigas
Diet: Nectar from flowers such as goldenrods and asters

BLUE MORPHO *(MORPHO MENELAUS)*

Blue morphos have vivid blue wings, and males are more brightly colored than females. The wings have brown undersides with many spots, some of which look like eyes. When the wings are closed, the brown color and spots help hide blue morphos from predators such as birds. These butterflies spend most of their time on the rain forest floor. They can also be spotted flying along the edges of streams and rivers.

HOW TO SPOT

Size: Wingspan of 5 to 8 inches (12.7 to 20.3 cm)

Range: Central America to Colombia

Habitat: Tropical rain forests

Diet: Rotting fruits, tree sap, fungi, mud, and fluids from dead animals

FUN FACT

Pilots flying over rain forests have spotted groups of blue morphos high above the treetops, warming themselves in the sun.

BLUE MOTHER-OF-PEARL
(SALAMIS TEMORA)

Blue mother-of-pearl butterflies have bright bluish-purple wings with black dots near the borders. The hindwings have yellow-brown borders with black dots and eyespots. The undersides of the wings are brown with eyespots. The brown color helps them blend in with dead leaves and tree bark in the forest. This camouflage helps hide the butterflies from predators.

HOW TO SPOT

Size: Wingspan of 3.1 to 3.5 inches (7.9 to 8.9 cm)

Range: Nigeria, Tanzania, Kenya, and Ethiopia

Habitat: Forests

Diet: Rotting fruits, mud puddles, dung, and carrion

COMMA *(POLYGONIA C-ALBUM)*

Comma butterflies have orange-brown wings with black spots. The underside of each wing is brown with a tiny white C mark that looks like a comma. The wings are jagged around the edges, which helps camouflage the butterfly. When resting on a tree branch with its head down and wings closed, the comma looks like a crinkled dead leaf.

FUN FACT

The comma butterfly and question mark butterfly are called the punctuation butterflies. That's because they both have markings on their wings that look like punctuation marks.

HOW TO SPOT

Size: Wingspan of 1.8 inches (4.6 cm)

Range: Europe, North Africa, Asia, and Japan

Habitat: Meadows, gardens, open woodlands, and forest edges

Diet: Tree sap, fruit juices from rotten fruits, and flower nectar from plants such as thistles

COMMON BUCKEYE *(JUNONIA COENIA)*

Common buckeyes have large, round eyespots on their wings to confuse predators. There are two eyespots on the forewings, along with two orange bars. Each hindwing has an orange margin close to the wing's edge and two eyespots. Common buckeyes often bask in open, sunny spaces. Adults fly quickly and low to the ground. Females lay single green eggs on the leaves of host plants.

HOW TO SPOT

Size: Wingspan of 2 to 2.5 inches (5 to 6.3 cm)
Range: Southern United States, Mexico, and the Caribbean
Habitat: Fields, gardens, parks, agricultural lands, scrubs, and pine savannas
Diet: Flower nectar

FUN FACT

The changing environment can trigger the common buckeye's color to shift. For instance, in the summer the undersides of the wings are brown. In the fall, they are reddish pink.

FOREST MONARCH
(TIRUMALA FORMOSA)

The forest monarch is also known as the beautiful monarch. Its black body is speckled with white dots. Its wings are mostly dark brown and have white spots. The lower part of each forewing is brownish orange. As caterpillars, these insects eat plants that make them poisonous to predators as adults.

HOW TO SPOT

Size: Wingspan of 3.5 inches (8.9 cm)
Range: Africa
Habitat: Tropical forests
Diet: Flower nectar

MIMICRY

The regal swallowtail looks very similar to the forest monarch. The regal swallowtail is not poisonous, but because it looks like the toxic forest monarch, predators stay away from both butterflies. One species copying the color and pattern of another is called mimicry.

GLASSWING BUTTERFLY
(GRETA OTO)

Glasswing butterflies have transparent wings with brown edges, dark veins, and some coloring on the tips of their wings. The transparent wings are a form of camouflage. The wings are clear like glass, which helps these butterflies blend in with their surroundings. Even though their wings look delicate, these butterflies are strong fliers and can travel long distances. Predators have a hard time spotting this butterfly's clear wings when it flies.

FUN FACT

Female glasswing butterflies lay their eggs on plants from the nightshade family. The caterpillars eat these toxic plants. Both the caterpillars and adult butterflies are poisonous.

HOW TO SPOT

Size: Wingspan of 2.1 to 2.3 inches (5.3 to 5.8 cm)

Range: Central and South America

Habitat: Tropical rain forests

Diet: Nectar from flowers such as lantanas

MANGROVE BUCKEYE
(JUNONIA GENOVEVA)

Mangrove buckeyes are reddish brown. They have orange stripes on their forewings and hindwings. The wings also have large eyespots, which scare away predators such as small birds. Females tend to be larger than males and have rounder forewings. Mangrove buckeyes have light-colored antennae with black or brown tips. These insects live together in small groups of ten to 20 butterflies.

HOW TO SPOT

Size: Wingspan of 1.4 to 2.2 inches (3.6 to 5.6 cm)

Range: Southern Florida, Mexico's Atlantic coast, and the Caribbean islands

Habitat: Open areas, roadsides, park trails, forest edges, and black mangrove swamps

Diet: Flower nectar

MONARCH *(DANAUS PLEXIPPUS)*

Monarchs are large butterflies with bright-orange wings. Black veins run through the wings, and white spots dot the edges. The undersides of the monarch's wings are pale orange. During its caterpillar stage, this insect eats milkweed. This makes the adult monarch poisonous to predators. Its bright-orange color is a warning to predators that it is toxic.

HOW TO SPOT

Size: Wingspan of 3 to 4 inches (7.6 to 10.2 cm)

Range: North and South America, Australia, New Zealand, parts of southern Europe and Asia, and the Canary Islands

Habitat: Gardens, meadows, grasslands, forests, and mountains

Diet: Flower nectar from blooming native plants, including milkweeds

FUN FACT

Most adult monarchs live between four and five weeks.

MONARCH MIGRATION

Each fall, monarchs migrate thousands of miles to escape the cold weather. In North America, there are two populations of monarchs separated by the Rocky Mountains. The population east of the Rocky Mountains flies to central Mexico for the winter. The western population travels to coastal California. Around March, monarchs fly north. It takes three to five generations of monarchs to reach the United States and southern Canada in late summer.

MOURNING CLOAK
(NYMPHALIS ANTIOPA)

Mourning cloaks have dark-maroon wings with yellowish borders. Along the borders are blue spots. When its wings are closed, the butterfly looks like a dead leaf. Males perch in open clearings on sunny afternoons and wait to mate with females. Mourning cloaks are seen from March to August in areas with willow trees, which are a popular food for mourning cloak caterpillars. These butterflies are strong fliers.

HOW TO SPOT

Size: Wingspan of 2.3 to 4 inches (5.8 to 10.2 cm)

Range: North America and Europe

Habitat: Woods, parks, and suburbs

Diet: Tree sap, rotting fruits, and sometimes flower nectar

OWL BUTTERFLY *(CALIGO MEMNON)*

The owl butterfly is one of the largest butterflies in the world. It is also known as the giant owl or pale owl. These butterflies have unique color patterns. Their forewings are creamy brown with brown borders. The hindwings are brownish black. The underwings are brown and gray. Each underwing has a large spot that looks like an owl eye. This butterfly is active at dawn and dusk.

HOW TO SPOT

Size: Wingspan of 4.8 to 5.3 inches (12.2 to 13.5 cm)

Range: Central and South America

Habitat: Tropical rain forests

Diet: Rotting fruits and animal dung

FOOLING PREDATORS

When owl butterflies close their wings, predators see large eyespots. The eyespots confuse predators. They might bite the eyespots, thinking they've found the butterfly's head. Owl butterflies can still fly away even if part of a wing is missing.

PAINTED LADY *(VANESSA CARDUI)*

Painted ladies are the most widespread butterflies in the world and can be found on almost every continent. These butterflies have brown and orange forewings. Their black wingtips have white spots. The undersides of the hindwings have small spots near the edges. Painted ladies sometimes have a small area of blue coloring on each hindwing. These butterflies are able to travel great distances.

HOW TO SPOT

Size: Wingspan of 2 to 2.9 inches (5 to 7.4 cm)

Range: Every continent except Australia and Antarctica

Habitat: Open areas such as meadows, gardens, and vacant lots

Diet: Flower nectar, especially from thistles

FUN FACT

The painted lady is a strong and fast flier. It can fly up to 620 miles (1,000 km) at a speed of 9 miles per hour (14 kmh).

QUEEN *(DANAUS GILIPPUS)*

The tops of the queen butterfly's forewings are brownish orange with two rows of white spots on a black border. White spots are also scattered across the tops of the forewings. The underside of each hindwing has black veins with two rows of white spots on a black border. Caterpillars eat milkweeds, and adult queens sip nectar from these plants. Milkweed has a toxin that stays in both the caterpillar and adult queen butterfly, making them taste bad to predators such as birds.

FUN FACT

The queen butterfly is similar in size and appearance to the monarch. It's easiest to tell the two butterflies apart when their wings are open. Monarchs have black veins on the tops of their wings, which queens do not have. Queens have black veins only on the undersides of their hindwings.

HOW TO SPOT

Size: Wingspan of 2.6 to 3.9 inches (6.6 to 10 cm)

Range: Africa, Asia, southern United States through the West Indies, and Central America to Argentina

Habitat: Places where milkweeds are found in open areas, including meadows, fields, deserts, marshes, and woodlands

Diet: Nectar from milkweeds, frog fruits, beggar's ticks, mistflowers, and lantanas

QUESTION MARK
(POLYGONIA INTERROGATIONIS)

The question mark is a red-orange butterfly with black spots. Its wings have an almost ragged look, and each upper forewing has a dramatic curve on the side. Question marks have dark hindwings in the summer and orange hindwings in the winter. These butterflies have light-brown undersides with tiny white colorings that look like question marks. In the summer, part of each hindwing is black with a short tail. In winter, part of each hindwing is orange with a purple-tipped tail.

HOW TO SPOT

Size: Wingspan of 2 to 2.5 inches (5 to 6.3 cm)

Range: Eastern United States, southern Canada, and central Mexico

Habitat: Open wooded areas, parks, and suburbs

Diet: Rotting fruits, tree sap, dung, carrion, and sometimes nectar

RED ADMIRAL *(VANESSA ATALANTA)*

Each of the red admiral's forewings is black with white spots near the wing tips. The butterfly gets its name from the prominent red-orange stripe across its forewings. The hindwings have red-orange markings with black spots and small, blue patches. The red admiral is a strong and fast flier. Males defend their territories and often chase away rival butterflies. Red admirals mate from late spring to early summer. Like some other butterflies, red admirals get water and minerals from muddy puddles, tree sap, and dung.

FUN FACT
Red admirals are often larger and more colorful in the summer than in the winter.

HOW TO SPOT

Size: Wingspan of 1.8 to 3 inches (4.6 to 7.6 cm)
Range: North and Central America, Europe, Asia, Australia, and Africa
Habitat: Yards, parks, wet fields, marshes, and woods
Diet: Flower nectar, mud, tree sap, and dung

REGAL FRITILLARY *(SPEYERIA IDALIA)*

The regal fritillary has mostly orange and black coloring.
Males have orange forewings with black markings, and
their hindwings are brownish orange with orange and
white spots. Females have orange forewings with black
markings and some white spots, and their hindwings
are brown or black with cream spots. These butterflies
used to be widespread in the United States, but over the
years their numbers have declined dramatically. The regal
fritillary needs prairie land to survive, but that habitat has
decreased in the United States due to human activities.

HOW TO SPOT

Size: Wingspan of 2.6 to 4.1 inches (6.6 to 10.4 cm)

Range: Montana, eastern North Dakota to Colorado,
Nebraska, and Oklahoma

Habitat: Tallgrass prairies

Diet: Nectar from flowers such as milkweeds, thistles,
blazing stars, and purple coneflowers

SILVER EMPEROR *(DOXOCOPA LAURE)*

Male and female silver emperors have slightly different colors on their wings. Males have brown forewings with orange stripes and a bit of blue. Females' forewings are brown with white stripes and yellow spots at the wingtips. Both males and females have brown hindwings with white bands and some blue on them. The undersides of the wings for both sexes are grayish silver. The butterfly's coloring helps camouflage it from predators, especially when it's on the ground.

Male

HOW TO SPOT

Size: Wingspan of 2.8 to 3.1 inches (7 to 7.9 cm)
Range: Southern United States and northern Mexico to Brazil
Habitat: Wooded areas and edges
Diet: Rotting fruits, sap, dung, and dead animals

SOLDIER *(DANAUS ERESIMUS)*

Soldier butterflies have orange wings with black veins, black borders, and white spots. They look similar to monarch and queen butterflies. However, soldiers are smaller than monarchs and have darker-orange wings, and soldiers have veins on their forewings that queens lack. Like both the monarch and queen, the soldier butterfly uses milkweed as a host plant for its caterpillars. It can be spotted in southern Texas from August to December and year-round in Florida.

HOW TO SPOT

Size: Wingspan of 2.8 to 3.8 inches (7 to 9.7 cm)

Range: Southern United States, the West Indies, and Central America into Brazil

Habitat: Pastures, fields, and edges of tropical forests in the dry season

Diet: Flower nectar

FUN FACT
The soldier flies and moves slowly, so it can be easily spotted and approached.

VARIABLE CRACKER
(HAMADRYAS FERONIA)

The variable cracker is a brown-and-white butterfly, sometimes bluish, with a small, red-orange bar on each forewing. Each hindwing has brown and white coloring and is dotted with eyespots. The butterfly's coloring helps it blend in with tree trunks and the forest ground. This camouflage allows the variable cracker to escape the notice of predators.

HOW TO SPOT

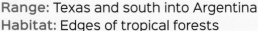

Size: Wingspan of 2.8 to 3.3 inches (7 to 8.4 cm)
Range: Texas and south into Argentina
Habitat: Edges of tropical forests
Diet: Decaying fruits and dung

BUTTERFLY SOUNDS

The variable cracker gets its name from the clicking noises it makes with its wings while flying. In 1874, the famous naturalist Charles Darwin thought the butterflies might use these clicking sounds to attract mates. Other experts wondered if the sounds were used to scare away predators. The butterflies often make these sounds when bothered by other animals. In addition, scientists know the butterflies can hear the clicking noises, so the butterflies could be communicating with one another.

VICEROY *(LIMENITIS ARCHIPPUS)*

Viceroy butterflies have orange wings with black veins and borders and white spots. The viceroy looks very similar to the monarch, but the viceroy has a black stripe across each hindwing. The viceroy is poisonous and tastes very bad to predators. In late morning and early afternoon, males search for females and defend their territories. Viceroys prefer to live in wet habitats.

HOW TO SPOT

Size: Wingspan of 2.5 to 3.4 inches (6.3 to 8.6 cm)

Range: North America

Habitat: Along ponds, swamps, rivers, meadows, and marshes

Diet: Flower nectar, decaying fruits, carrion, and dung

FUN FACT

The viceroy and monarch display mimicry with each other. These similar-looking butterflies are toxic, which keeps predators away from both of them.

WHITE ADMIRAL *(LIMENITIS CAMILLA)*

White admirals have black wings with large, white stripes across them. The undersides of the wings have orange-brown, white, and black markings. These butterflies are active from mid-June to mid-August, with the largest numbers spotted in July. White admirals are often found high in treetops. They live for about two weeks.

HOW TO SPOT

Size: Wingspan of 2.4 inches (6 cm)

Range: Europe and Asia

Habitat: Forests

Diet: Nectar from brambles

ZEBRA LONGWING
(HELICONIUS CHARITHONIA)

Zebra longwing butterflies have long wings and bold patterns. The wings are black with several yellow stripes. The undersides of the wings have a similar pattern but are lighter in color with small, red spots near the body. The zebra longwing can be seen year-round in tropical forests. Females lay eggs on host plants from the passionflower family. The zebra's bold, striped pattern warns predators that this butterfly is toxic and to avoid it.

FUN FACT
The zebra longwing was named Florida's state butterfly in 1996.

HOW TO SPOT

Size: Wingspan of 2.8 to 4 inches (7 to 10.2 cm)
Range: Southern parts of the United States, Central America, South America, and the West Indies
Habitat: Tropical forests
Diet: Flower nectar and pollen

EATING POLLEN

The zebra butterfly sips flower nectar. But unlike other butterflies, the zebra also feeds on pollen. Pollen is very nutritious because it is rich in protein. This differs from nectar, which is mainly sugar. As a result of feeding on pollen, the zebra lives longer than other butterflies. Many butterflies have a life span of two to four weeks, but the zebra can live and lay eggs for several months.

ADONIS BLUE
(POLYOMMATUS BELLARGUS)

Male Adonis blues have blue wings. Females are brown with a bluish hue toward the base of their wings. The undersides of both males and females are brown with orange and white-and-black spots. The female's brown color allows it to escape the notice of predators. When predators spot a male, the butterfly goes to the ground and closes its wings. With its wings closed, the butterfly blends in with the ground.

HOW TO SPOT

Size: Wingspan of 1.2 inches (3 cm)

Range: Europe and Central Asia

Habitat: Grasslands and meadows

Diet: Flower nectar and dung

Male

A SWEET RELATIONSHIP WITH ANTS

Adonis blue caterpillars have a relationship with ants. The ants feed on a sugary substance produced by the caterpillars. In return, the ants protect the caterpillars from other insects. At night, the ants cover the caterpillars with a thin layer of soil and stand guard over them.

AMERICAN COPPER
(LYCAENA PHLAEAS)

The American copper is also known as the little copper or small copper. The upper side of each forewing is orange with black spots and has a gray-brown border. Each hindwing is grayish brown and has an orange stripe near the edge, along with a row of black spots. The forewings' undersides are pale orange with black spots. The underside of each hindwing is white with black spots and an orange line.

HOW TO SPOT

Size: Wingspan of 1 to 1.3 inches (2.5 to 3.3 cm)

Range: Northern and central North America, Europe, Asia, and northern Africa

Habitat: Fields, prairies, landfills, rocky areas in the Rocky Mountains, alpine fields in the Sierra Nevada, and Arctic tundra

Diet: Nectar from flowers such as common buttercups, clovers, yarrows, butterfly weeds, blazing stars, wild strawberries, and mountain mints

FUN FACT

The American copper is active from early morning to dusk. It basks in the sun and rests on tall flowers such as daisies. This butterfly is very aggressive. Males patrol their territories and quickly chase away other butterflies.

BANDED HAIRSTREAK
(SATYRIUM CALANUS)

Banded hairstreaks have gray wings with white and black markings. Each hindwing has a blue patch, an orange eyespot, and both a long and short tail. In early summer, males perch in sunny, open areas in the forest and wait for females. Females lay eggs on the twigs of host plants such as oak, walnut, and hickory trees.

HOW TO SPOT

Size: Wingspan of about 1 inch (2.5 cm)

Range: Central Canada and central and eastern United States down to Florida

Habitat: Forests, forest edges, and fields

Diet: Nectar from flowers including dogbane, milkweeds, New Jersey tea, and meadowsweet

FUN FACT
The best time to see female banded hairstreaks is in the early morning or late afternoon as they sip nectar from flowers.

MALES SQUARE OFF

Male banded hairstreaks are known for skirmishing with one other. They fly from their perches, flutter around each other, and defend their territories. The clashes can last several minutes. Sometimes, the males might pause and then go after each other again. After the skirmish, the males return to their perches.

BRONZE COPPER *(LYCAENA HYLLUS)*

Male and female bronze coppers have different appearances. The upper sides of males' wings are brown with a purplish tint, while females' wings are copper colored with dark spots. Both males and females have an orange stripe across each hindwing. In addition, the undersides of the forewings are orange. The underside of each hindwing is light gray with an orange stripe and black dots.

HOW TO SPOT

Size: Wingspan of 1.3 to 1.9 inches (3.3 to 4.8 cm)
Range: Southern Canada and the United States
Habitat: Wetlands and wetland edges
Diet: Nectar from flowers such as swamp milkweed and goldenrods

FUN FACT
Bronze coppers are food for sparrows and bluebirds. Crab spiders and assassin bugs also attack bronze coppers as the butterflies sip nectar from flowers.

BROWN ELFIN
(CALLOPHRYS AUGUSTINUS)

Brown elfin males have gray to brown wings with dark patches on their forewings. Females have red-brown wings. For both sexes, the undersides of the wings are brown and become darker toward the base. The underside also has a line of black spots across the middle. Neither males nor females have tails.

HOW TO SPOT

Size: Wingspan of 1 to 1.3 inches (2.5 to 3.3 cm)

Range: Canada and the northern United States to Alabama and California

Habitat: Sagebrush steppes, chaparrals, forests, forest edges, roadsides, yards, gardens, parks, bogs, and open areas in mountains

Diet: Flower nectar

FUN FACT
The male brown elfin perches on plants during the day and can also be found along paths and stream banks. The female lays eggs on a variety of host plants, including blueberries and huckleberries.

CHALK HILL BLUE
(LYSANDRA CORIDON)

Male chalk hill blues have blue wings with dark-brown edges and white fringes. These colorful wings help attract females. Under the bright sun, the male's wings look silver. Females have brown wings with blue edging. The duller-brown color helps females blend into their surroundings and hide from predators. Chalk hill blues are active from July to September. At dusk, the butterflies gather at the bottoms of hills and roost overnight in tall grasses.

HOW TO SPOT

Size: Wingspan of 1.4 inches (3.6 cm)
Range: Sections of Europe and western Asia
Habitat: Chalk and limestone grasslands
Diet: Nectar from flowers such as thistles and knapweeds; occasionally animal dung

Male

Female

SERENADING ANTS

A chalk hill blue caterpillar forms its chrysalis on the ground. The chrysalis produces substances that attract ants. The ants cover the chrysalis with soil to protect it from other insects. Before the chalk hill blue emerges from the chrysalis, it makes noises to attract the ants. In response, the ants gather around the chrysalis and protect the emerging adult butterfly from other insects and from arachnids.

37

COMMON IMPERIAL BLUE
(JALMENUS EVAGORAS)

Common imperial blues have blue coloring and black borders on their wings. Each forewing has a small, black bar near the top. The hindwings have two orange spots and white lines. Each hindwing also has a tail. Common imperial blues have cream to brown undersides with black lines, orange-brown stripes and markings, and orange spots near the tails. Females lay clusters of eggs on different kinds of acacia trees and shrubs. Caterpillars and their chrysalises produce sugary substances that ants feed on. In return, the ants protect the caterpillars and chrysalises from predators.

FUN FACT

When common imperial blues rest, their tails move back and forth like antennae. Predators are confused by this. They may bite the tails, thinking they are the butterfly's head.

HOW TO SPOT

Size: Wingspan of 1.5 inches (3.8 cm)
Range: Australia
Habitat: Edges of forests and roadsides where acacia trees and shrubs grow
Diet: Nectar from flowering bushes and shrubs

CORAL HAIRSTREAK
(SATYRIUM TITUS)

Coral hairstreaks are one of the largest and most common hairstreak butterflies. The upper sides of their wings are brown, and the undersides are a lighter brown gray. The underside of each hindwing has a row of black spots surrounded by white. The edge of each hindwing has a row of orange spots. Unlike some other hairstreaks, this butterfly does not have a tail. The coral hairstreak is most active during a few weeks in early summer.

HOW TO SPOT

Size: Wingspan of 1 to 1.5 inches (2.5 to 3.8 cm)
Range: Eastern California, southern United States, and British Columbia
Habitat: Brushy areas and overgrown fields
Diet: Nectar from plants including butterfly weed, dogbane, and New Jersey tea

EASTERN TAILED BLUE
(CUPIDO COMYNTAS)

Male eastern tailed blues have blue wings with black borders and white fringes on the edges. Females have dark, brownish wings. In the spring, some blue will appear near the base of the wings. The upper sides of the hindwings in both males and females have one or two orange spots near the tails. The undersides of the butterfly's wings are silver with black dashes and dots. There are also one to three orange spots on each hindwing.

Male

HOW TO SPOT

Size: Wingspan of 0.8 to 1.1 inches (2 to 2.8 cm)

Range: Eastern North America and south to Costa Rica

Habitat: Gardens, roadsides, fields, meadows, and parks

Diet: Puddles for water and flower nectar

FUN FACT
Females lay eggs on young flower buds. That way, when the caterpillars hatch, they will have a young flower to feed on.

Female

GRAY HAIRSTREAK
(STRYMON MELINUS)

Gray hairstreaks are the most common hairstreak in North America. Their wings are gray with an orange spot and tail on each hindwing. The undersides of the wings are light gray. There is a line of white, black, and orange dashes. There's also an orange area near the tail. This butterfly basks in the sun with its wings open. Males perch on trees and shrubs and wait for females. The caterpillars aren't picky and eat a wide variety of plants.

HOW TO SPOT

Size: Wingspan of 1.5 inches (3.8 cm)

Range: United States and southern Canada

Habitat: Open areas such as fields, roadsides, gardens, and parks

Diet: Nectar from flowers such as large daisies, dogbane, milkweeds, mints, asters, and clovers

GREAT PURPLE HAIRSTREAK
(ATLIDES HALESUS)

Great purple hairstreaks are large butterflies with wings that are black and bright blue. Males are slightly brighter than females. The undersides of the wings are purplish black. Each hindwing has one long tail and one short tail. The butterfly's abdomen is red-orange underneath and blue on the top. The great purple hairstreak is active from spring to fall and nearly year-round in southern Florida. The female lays its eggs on mistletoe, which the caterpillars eat when they emerge.

FUN FACT
Male great purple hairstreaks attract females by fluttering their wings vigorously.

HOW TO SPOT

Size: Wingspan of 1.3 to 2 inches (3.3 to 5 cm)
Range: Southern North America and Central America
Habitat: Woodlands
Diet: Nectar from flowers such as desert lavender

GREEN HAIRSTREAK
(CALLOPHRYS RUBI)

The green hairstreak has brown wings on its upper side. The underside is green with a white stripe along the margin of the forewings and hindwings. This butterfly can be spotted from April to June within its range. It rests with its wings closed. The male green hairstreak aggressively defends its territory, chasing away other insects.

HOW TO SPOT

Size: Wingspan of 1 to 1.4 inches (2.5 to 3.6 cm)
Range: Europe, North Africa, and Asia
Habitat: Moors, hillsides, and valley bottoms
Diet: Nectar from a wide variety of herbs and bushes

JUNIPER HAIRSTREAK
(CALLOPHRYS GRYNEUS)

In the eastern part of its range, the male juniper hairstreak has dark-brown wings with a greenish hue. Females have dark-brown wings. The undersides of the wings are green in both males and females. Each hindwing has two white spots and a zigzagging white line edged with red brown.

In the western part of its range, the upper sides of the male's wings are red brown and the female has light-brown wings. The undersides are brownish red. Each hindwing has a zigzagging white line surrounded with a red-brown color.

HOW TO SPOT

Size: Wingspan of 0.8 to 1 inches (2 to 2.5 cm)

Range: British Columbia, the United States, and northern Mexico

Habitat: Areas where cedar and juniper plants are found, including woodlands and bluffs

Diet: Nectar from flowers including winter cress, dogbane, common milkweed, butterfly weed, and white sweet clover

KARNER BLUE
(LYCAEIDES MELISSA SAMUELIS)

Male and female Karner blue butterflies have different appearances. Males have dark-blue wings with black margins and white, fringed edges. Females are dark blue to gray brown. They have orange markings on their hindwings. In both males and females, the undersides of the wings are gray with black spots. They also have orange markings and silvery spots near the edges. Karner blues are active from early morning to early evening. When it becomes too hot, the butterflies rest in the shade.

FUN FACT
Female Karner blue butterflies lay light-green eggs on sticks, pebbles, blades of grasses, and lupine plants.

HOW TO SPOT

Size: Wingspan of 1 inch (2.5 cm)

Range: Midwestern United States, New Hampshire, and New York

Habitat: Pine barrens, oak savannas, and lakeshore dunes where wild lupine plants grow

Diet: Nectar from flowers, including butterfly weed, leafy spurge, blazing stars, wild Virginia strawberries, and New Jersey tea

Female

LARGE GREEN-BANDED BLUE
(DANIS DANIS)

The large green-banded blue is a tropical butterfly. Males have blue wings with large, white stripes and black edges. Females have black wings with white stripes and bluish hues near the base. In both males and females, the undersides of the wings have white and blue coloring. They also have black margins, black dots, and light-green bands. These butterflies usually spend their time in shady rain forest areas, but they can be found resting on sunny leaves now and then.

HOW TO SPOT

Size: Wingspan of 1.5 to 1.8 inches (3.8 to 4.6 cm)
Range: Australia, New Guinea, and the Philippines
Habitat: Tropical rain forests
Diet: Nectar from flowers such as lantanas

PURPLISH COPPER
(LYCAENA HELLOIDES)

Purplish copper males have brown wings with purplish highlights and black spots. Each hindwing has an orange stripe near the edge. Females have orange wings with black markings. In both males and females, the undersides of the wings are light gray or orange with black dots, and there's an orange stripe on the edge of each hindwing. The purplish copper can be spotted from May to September at low elevations and from July to August at higher elevations.

HOW TO SPOT

Size: Wingspan of 1.5 inches (3.8 cm)
Range: Canada and the western to upper midwestern United States
Habitat: Meadows, valleys, and stream banks
Diet: Nectar from flowers such as asters, thistles, Queen Anne's lace, and goldenrods

FUN FACT
The purplish copper is the most widespread copper butterfly in the western United States.

Male

SMALL BROWN AZURE
(OGYRIS OTANES)

Both male and female small brown azures have purple coloring on their wings. The female also has a black band and white area near the top of each forewing. The undersides of both males and females are brown to gray with black spots. In addition, the underside of each lower forewing has two black-and-white spots. The small brown azure can be spotted from October to April. Males gather on the ground or on hilltops and bask in the morning sun. They feed on flower nectar and set up territories to watch for females. Females feed on flower nectar in the early morning before mating. They lay eggs at the bottom of host plants.

HOW TO SPOT

Size: Wingspan of 1.5 inches (3.8 cm)

Range: Southern Australia

Habitat: Dry grasslands, scrubs, and dry woodlands

Diet: Nectar from low-growing, flowering shrubs in the rice flower family

Female

DISAPPEARING FROM AUSTRALIA

The small brown azure was once common in southern Australia but is now a rare butterfly. Some reasons for its decline include the clearing of native plants that the butterfly depends on, bush fires, and toxic sprays used on agricultural lands.

SPRING AZURE *(CELASTRINA LADON)*

The spring azure is a small butterfly. Males have purple-blue wings with black borders. Females are light blue or white with black bands on the forewings and hindwings. The undersides of the wings in both males and females are white to gray with black dots, dashes, and squiggly lines. The spring azure flies close to the ground and likes to bask in the warm sun. The males watch for females and gather on mud puddles.

Male

HOW TO SPOT

Size: Wingspan of 0.9 to 1.4 inches (2.3 to 3.6 cm)

Range: Eastern United States

Habitat: Forests, gardens, fields, pastures, wetlands, and swamps

Diet: Mud, dung, and nectar from flowers such as viburnums, New Jersey tea, dogbane, common milkweed, and blackberries

FUN FACT

The spring azure is active from May to August in the northern part of its range and from January to October in the southern part.

WESTERN PYGMY BLUE
(BREPHIDIUM EXILIS)

The western pygmy blue is the smallest butterfly in North America. Its wings are brown with blue near the base and white on the edges. The undersides of the wings are brown with gray at the base and black spots on the border of each hindwing. The western pygmy blue is a weak-flying butterfly. It flies slowly and close to the ground. It is found year-round in the southern part of its range. The fall season is a good time to spot groups of western pygmy blues together.

HOW TO SPOT

Size: Wingspan of 0.5 to 0.6 inches (1.3 to 1.5 cm)

Range: California to Mexico, and Hawaii

Habitat: Gardens, salt marshes, desert salt flats, and woods

Diet: Flower nectar

WHITE LETTER HAIRSTREAK
(SATYRIUM W-ALBUM)

The white letter hairstreak's name comes from the white markings on the underside of its wings that look like the letter *W*. The tops of the butterfly's wings are dark brown. The undersides are light brown with an orange band near the wing edges. The white letter hairstreak is active from July to August. It is a difficult butterfly to spot because it spends most of its time flying high in the treetops. Small groups often gather on a few trees or a single tree.

HOW TO SPOT

Size: Wingspan of 1 to 1.4 inches (2.5 to 3.6 cm)

Range: Europe and Asia

Habitat: Forests

Diet: Nectar from flowers such as brambles and privets, and a sugary liquid called honeydew made by aphids

DUTCH ELM DISEASE

The white letter hairstreak's numbers have been drastically reduced in the United Kingdom due to Dutch elm disease, a disease that kills all types of elm trees. This butterfly depends on elm trees as part of its life cycle. Since the mid-1970s, more than 30 million elm trees have died from Dutch elm disease. As a result, the white letter hairstreak population has declined by 96 percent in the United Kingdom.

LITTLE METALMARK
(CALEPHELIS VIRGINIENSIS)

Little metalmarks are small butterflies with orange-brown or rusty-orange wings with silver lines. The undersides of their wings are a brighter orange. The little metalmark flies low to the ground and rests with its wings open. Males patrol small areas to search for females. Females lay single eggs on the undersides of host plant leaves, which include herbs such as yellow thistle and vanilla leaf.

HOW TO SPOT

Size: Wingspan of 0.5 to 1 inch (1.3 to 2.5 cm)

Range: Southeastern United States

Habitat: Wetlands, dunes, pine savannas, and pra[...]

Diet: N[...] r from flowers such as yarrow and bl[...] nist

MORMON METALMARK
(APODEMIA MORMO)

Mormon metalmarks have orange-brown to black wings with many white spots. The top of each forewing has a reddish-orange patch. The undersides of the hindwings are gray with white markings. This butterfly zips along quickly. It is active from July to September in the northern part of its range and from March to October in the southern region.

HOW TO SPOT

Size: Wingspan of 0.8 to 1.3 inches (2 to 3.3 cm)

Range: Southern Canada, the western United States, and northern Mexico

Habitat: Grasslands, chaparrals, woodlands, dunes, roadsides, hillsides, and rocky slopes

Diet: Flower nectar

FUN FACT
The Mormon metalmark butterfly lives only nine to days.

NORTHERN METALMARK
(CALEPHELIS BOREALIS)

Northern metalmarks have red-brown to orange-brown wings. The wings also have silver-blue bands near the edges. The undersides of the wings are bright yellow orange with black markings and shiny, silver lines near the edges. Males perch on leaves and watch for females. Females lay eggs one at a time underneath leaves. This butterfly flies only short distances, so it stays in areas with plenty of food.

FUN FACT
Northern metalmarks rest upside down underneath leaves.

HOW TO SPOT

Size: Wingspan of 1.1 to 1.3 inches (2.8 to 3.3 cm)

Range: Eastern United States

Habitat: Stream banks and meadows near forests

Diet: Nectar from flowers such as butterfly weed, white sweet clover, goldenrods, oxeye daisies, yarrow, and black-eyed Susans

LOSING ITS HOME

There are small, isolated populations of northern metalmarks in Connecticut, Pennsylvania, the central Appalachians, the Ohio River Valley, Missouri, and Oklahoma. This butterfly's range used to be much larger. The population has declined because the butterfly's habitat is being destroyed. Urban development, pesticide use, and invasive plants eliminate the plants and flowers these butterflies depend on for survival.

RED-BORDERED METALMARK
(CARIA INO)

Male red-bordered metalmarks have dark-brown wings with orange borders and a silver line near the edges of the wings. Females have light-orange wings. The undersides of the wings in both males and females are reddish orange with silver markings and black spots. This butterfly is active from spring to fall.

HOW TO SPOT

Size: Wingspan of 0.8 to 1 inch (2 to 2.5 cm)

Range: Southern Texas and south to Costa Rica

Habitat: Subtropical forests

Diet: Flower nectar

Male

RED-BORDERED PIXIE
(MELANIS PIXE)

Red-bordered pixies have black wings with red spots at the base of the forewings. The tips of the forewings are yellow orange. Each hindwing has a band of red spots near the edge. The undersides of the wings have a similar pattern. The red-bordered pixie is active in the early morning or on cloudy days for most of the year. It avoids bright sunshine. Females lay eggs in clusters of ten to 30 on tree leaves, branches, or bark. Food plants for the caterpillars include Guamuchil trees.

HOW TO SPOT

Size: Wingspan of 1.5 to 1.9 inches (3.8 to 4.8 cm)

Range: Lower Rio Grande Valley of Texas and south to Costa Rica

Habitat: Tropical forests and city parks

Diet: Flower nectar

SWAMP METALMARK
(CALEPHELIS MUTICUM)

Swamp metalmarks have red-brown wings with two rows of wavy, silver lines. The undersides of their wings are light yellow to brown with black dots and silver specks. The swamp metalmark is active from mid-July to mid-August. It flies slowly and low to the ground. This is a rare and endangered butterfly across its range.

HOW TO SPOT

Size: Wingspan of 1 to 1.3 inches (2.5 to 3.3 cm)

Range: United States, including Iowa, Wisconsin, Michigan, Missouri, Ohio, Kentucky, and northern Arkansas

Habitat: Wet, open areas where swamp thistles grow

Diet: Nectar from flowers including black-eyed Susan, swamp thistle, swamp milkweed, mountain mint, meadowsweet, and yarrow

FUN FACT
In 2011, a photographer discovered a swamp metalmark at a nature preserve in northwest Alabama, approximately 300 miles (480 km) away from the nearest known population.

SAVING WETLAND BUTTERFLIES

The swamp metalmark's caterpillars eat only one food plant: swamp thistles. Swamp thistles are getting crowded out by invasive plant species, which makes it difficult for the caterpillars to survive and flourish. The Toledo Zoo in Ohio has a butterfly project to save wetland butterflies, including the swamp metalmark. The zoo grows food plants for the caterpillars. It also raises the butterflies and releases them into protected areas.

COMMON CHECKERED SKIPPER
(PYRGUS COMMUNIS)

Common checkered skippers have blue-gray hairs on their bodies. The male's wings are brownish with large, white spots. Females also have white spots, but their wings are darker. In both males and females, the undersides of the wings are white with gray or dark-green bands. The fast-flying common checkered skipper flits from flower to flower, sipping nectar. This insect can be spotted from February to October in the southern part of its range. In the northern part of its range, it is seen from March to September.

Male

Female

HOW TO SPOT

Size: Wingspan of 1 to 1.5 inches (2.5 to 3.8 cm)

Range: North America

Habitat: Meadows, fields, gardens, pastures, and roadsides

Diet: Nectar from flowers such as hollyhocks, mimosas, New England asters, and zinnias

DELAWARE SKIPPER

(ANATRYTONE LOGAN)

Delaware skippers have orange wings with black veins. The wings have black borders and orange fringes on the edges. The undersides of the wings are orange with no markings. These skippers are tricky to spot because they pass rapidly between flowers, sipping on nectar. Males perch on low grasses or along stream banks and watch for females to mate with. Females lay eggs one at a time on the leaves of host plants.

HOW TO SPOT

Size: Wingspan of 1 to 1.5 inches (2.5 to 3.8 cm)

Range: Midwestern and eastern North America to El Salvador

Habitat: Meadows, prairies, pond edges, marshes, bogs, pastures, parks, and gardens

Diet: Nectar from white and pink flowers including common milkweed, swamp milkweed, mountain mint, and thistles

FUN FACT

Delaware skippers rest with their forewings up in a V shape. Their hindwings stretch out horizontally on each side.

DINGY SKIPPER *(ERYNNIS TAGES)*

Dingy skippers have grayish-brown wings with brown markings and rows of tiny, white spots. The skipper's drab coloring helps it blend in well with its surroundings and provides excellent camouflage from predators. Adult dingy skippers can be spotted from May to the end of June within their range. If it's a warm spring, the adults might emerge as early as mid-April. This fast-flying insect stays close to the ground.

FUN FACT

Dingy skippers gather to roost overnight on dead flower heads. They wrap their wings around the dead flower heads while they rest.

HOW TO SPOT

Size: Wingspan of 1 inch (2.5 cm)
Range: Europe and Asia
Habitat: Grasslands, forest clearings, hillsides, dunes, and cliffs
Diet: Nectar from flowers such as bird's-foot trefoil, horseshoe vetch, buttercups, and hawkweed

DUN SKIPPER *(EUPHYES VESTRIS)*

Dun skippers have brownish-black wings, and females have a group of three or four small spots. The male's underside is brownish black. The female's underside is browner, and she has a few white spots there too. The dun skipper's head and thorax are yellowish orange to yellowish green. Females lay eggs one at a time on leaves of host plants. The eggs are green, but after a while a red spot and band appears on each egg.

Male

HOW TO SPOT

Size: Wingspan of 1.1 to 1.4 inches (2.8 to 3.6 cm)

Range: Southern Canada and the United States

Habitat: Meadows, pastures, fields, roadsides, marshes, and along creeks and streams

Diet: Nectar from white, pink, and purple flowers such as common milkweed, purple vetch, dogbane, and New Jersey tea

Female

ESSEX SKIPPER *(THYMELICUS LINEOLA)*

Essex skippers have orange wings with black borders and black veins. The undersides of the wings are orange brown. The antennae have black tips. The Essex skipper flies close to the ground. It basks in the sun during the day and roosts on tall grasses overnight. Adult Essex skippers can be spotted from May to July within their range.

HOW TO SPOT

Size: Wingspan of 1 to 1.3 inches (2.5 to 3.3 cm)
Range: North America, Europe, North Africa, and Asia
Habitat: Grasslands, meadows, and forests
Diet: Nectar from flowers such as thistles, clovers, and common fleabane

FUN FACT
Essex skippers gather in groups called colonies. These can range from just a few butterflies to thousands.

LARGE SKIPPER *(OCHLODES SYLVANUS)*

Large skippers have reddish-brown wings with light-orange spots and dark-brown edges. The male has a black stripe running across the centers of its forewings. In both males and females, the undersides of the wings have light-orange spots. This insect can be spotted in grassy areas where flowers grow from early June to mid-August.

HOW TO SPOT

Size: Wingspan of 1.1 to 1.4 inches (2.8 to 3.6 cm)

Range: Europe

Habitat: Meadows, hedgerows, roadsides, forest edges, parks, and gardens

Diet: Nectar from flowers such as brambles and thistles

Male

LEONARD'S SKIPPER
(HESPERIA LEONARDUS)

Leonard's skippers have reddish-orange wings with wide, black edges. The underside of each hindwing is a rusty red or orange color with white, cream, or yellow spots. This skipper can be seen flying between August and October. It flies quickly and beats its wings so rapidly that it appears as a blur. When resting in the sun, Leonard's skippers adjust their positions to make sure they don't overheat. They do this by partially opening their wings.

HOW TO SPOT

Size: Wingspan of 1.3 to 1.8 inches (3.3 to 4.6 cm)
Range: North America
Habitat: Prairies, fields, barrens, and meadows
Diet: Nectar from flowers such as blazing stars, thistles, and asters

LONG-TAILED SKIPPER
(URBANUS PROTEUS)

Long-tailed skippers have dark-brown wings with light-brown spots. The base of the wings is blue green. Underneath, the wings are light brown with dark markings. These skippers have hairy bodies and broad heads. The tops of their antennae are curved. Each hindwing has a long tail that is dark brown to black. Males and females perform courtship rituals where they spiral upward together, fall to the ground, and then mate.

HOW TO SPOT

Size: Wingspan of 1.8 to 2.3 inches (4.6 to 5.8 cm)

Range: Southern United States to Central America, the West Indies, and Argentina

Habitat: Forest edges, open fields, coastal dunes, and gardens

Diet: Nectar from flowers such as lantanas and shepherd's needles

FUN FACT

Long-tailed skippers lay eggs underneath bean plants. When too many larvae hatch at once, they can devastate farmers' bean crops.

NORTHERN CLOUDYWING
(THORYBES PYLADES)

Northern cloudywings have dark-brown wings with tiny spots. Underneath, the wings are brown with a dusting of gray toward the edges. The northern cloudywing is active in the north from spring to summer and from spring through fall in the southern part of its range. This insect perches and feeds with its wings spread open.

HOW TO SPOT

Size: Wingspan of 1.3 to 1.9 inches (3.3 to 4.8 cm)

Range: Canada to Mexico

Habitat: Fields, roadsides, savannas, and dry forests

Diet: Nectar from blue, pink, and white flowers such as verbena, dogbane, common milkweed, and clovers

SILVER-SPOTTED SKIPPER
(EPARGYREUS CLARUS)

The silver-spotted skipper is common across North America. It is easily recognizable by the large silvery-white patch on the underside of each hindwing. The tops of the skipper's wings are brown with yellow-orange coloring in the centers of the forewings. The silver-spotted skipper flies quickly and low to the ground as it darts between plants. This skipper usually perches with its wings closed. However, it might soak up the sun with its wings open in the early morning light.

FUN FACT
Larvae of silver-spotted skippers make leaf shelters. They hide in these and leave only to eat or to make even bigger shelters.

HOW TO SPOT

Size: Wingspan of 1.5 to 2.5 inches (3.8 to 6.3 cm)

Range: North America

Habitat: Forest edges, fields, gardens, roadsides, and pastures

Diet: Nectar from flowers such as buttonbush, milkweeds, thistles, verbena, zinnias, purple coneflowers, and clovers

SMALL SKIPPER
(THYMELICUS SYLVESTRIS)

Small skippers have orange wings with black borders and black veins near the edges. Underneath, the wings are orange brown. The male has a thin, black line across the center of each forewing. The small skipper emerges from its chrysalis in late June or early July and can be spotted in the summer. This skipper expertly darts through tall grasses and basks in the sun on top of tall grass blades.

HOW TO SPOT

Size: Wingspan of 1 to 1.3 inches (2.5 to 3.3 cm)

Range: Europe, northern Africa, and the Middle East

Habitat: Grasslands, roadsides, hedgerows, and woodland openings

Diet: Nectar from flowers including clovers, bird's-foot trefoil, vetch, thistles, knapweed, and oxeye daisies

FUN FACT
The small skipper looks incredibly similar to the Essex skipper. One way to tell them apart is to look at their antennae tips. The underside of the small skipper's antenna is dark red or orange. The underside of the Essex skipper's antenna is black.

AN UNUSUAL WAY TO LAY EGGS

The female small skipper lays its eggs by landing on top of a blade of grass. Then the skipper spins around and moves backward down the grass blade. It finds a slit in the grass and lays four or five eggs inside the grass stem.

SOUTHERN CLOUDYWING
(THORYBES BATHYLLUS)

The southern cloudywing is a medium-sized brown skipper. It has a row of light spots on the upper side of each forewing and a light-gray fringe on its wing edges. Underneath, this insect has two dark-brown stripes across the center of each hindwing. In the northern part of its range, the southern cloudywing can be spotted from mid-June to mid-July. In other parts of its range, the skipper is active from June to early October.

HOW TO SPOT

Size: Wingspan of 1.3 to 1.8 inches (3.3 to 4.6 cm)

Range: Eastern United States and Mexico

Habitat: Forest edges, roadsides, fields, gardens, dry meadows, and dry prairies

Diet: Nectar from flowers including dogbane, selfheal, crown vetch, thistles, and common milkweed

TAWNY-EDGED SKIPPER
(POLITES THEMISTOCLES)

Tawny-edged skippers have mostly brown wings, but the front edges of the forewings are orange. Underneath, the wings are gray and also have orange coloring. Females have a few white-orange spots on the upper side of each forewing. Tawny-edged skippers can be spotted in flight from May to late October in their range.

FUN FACT

Tawny-edged skippers are skilled at darting around grasses and between flowers, but predators such as harbor crab spiders, ambush bugs, robber flies, and praying mantises will attack them there.

HOW TO SPOT

Size: Wingspan of 1 to 1.3 inches (2.5 to 3.3 cm)

Range: Canada and the United States

Habitat: Meadows, prairies, fields, pastures, roadsides, and lawns

Diet: Nectar from flowers such as clovers, thistles, milkweeds, dogbane, mint, and asters

ZABULON SKIPPER
(POANES ZABULON)

Male zabulon skippers are orange with black bands on the tops of their wings. The undersides of the wings are yellow with brown dots. Females have purple-brown wings with light-yellow spots. The undersides of the female's wings are brown and purplish gray with white edges.

HOW TO SPOT

Size: Wingspan of 1.4 to 1.6 inches (3.6 to 4.1 cm)

Range: Midwestern to eastern United States and Central America

Habitat: Forests, streams, parks, and gardens

Diet: Nectar from flowers such as milkweeds, thistles, buttonbush, and joe-pye weed

Female

Male

71

APOLLO *(PARNASSIUS APOLLO)*

Apollos are large butterflies with white wings. They have black spots on the forewings and red to orange spots with white centers on the hindwings. The undersides of the wings have a similar pattern. The male is territorial and will chase away rival males from the area. Females lay eggs on stonecrops and houseleeks.

HOW TO SPOT

Size: Wingspan of 2.4 to 3.7 inches (6 to 9.4 cm)
Range: Europe and Asia
Habitat: Alpine meadows and pastures
Diet: Flower nectar

FUN FACT

Apollos live on open, rocky slopes that get plenty of sunshine. They prefer warm summers and cold winters.

THE DECLINE OF THE APOLLO

The number of Apollo butterflies has been dramatically declining since the 1970s. This is due to habitat loss and climate change. In addition, collectors often hunt down these insects, leading to the overcollection of these unique butterflies. The number of Apollos has declined by 20 to 50 percent in Europe.

BLACK SWALLOWTAIL
(PAPILIO POLYXENES)

Black swallowtails have black wings with two rows of yellow spots. They also have blue patches on their hindwings. The yellow spots are brighter and larger in males. The blue patches on the hindwings are more noticeable in females. Both males and females have a pair of red-orange spots between the tails on the hindwings. Underneath, the wings have rows of yellow-orange spots next to blue markings.

Female

HOW TO SPOT

Size: Wingspan of 2.7 to 3.3 inches (6.9 to 8.4 cm)

Range: Southern Canada, the United States, and northern Mexico

Habitat: Prairies, fields, woods, pine savannas, roadsides, weedy areas, and gardens

Diet: Nectar from flowers such as thistles and milkweeds

BROAD-BANDED SWALLOWTAIL
(PAPILIO ASTYALUS)

The broad-banded swallowtail is seen in its range between April and October. Males have large, yellow markings on their forewings. The hindwings have large, yellow spots along the wing borders. Each hindwing has a black tail. Females have dark-brown wings. Their hindwings have blue and orange bands with yellow spots and short tails. Males prefer open spaces, while females are often in wooded areas where they can lay eggs on citrus trees, which serve as host plants for the caterpillars.

Male

HOW TO SPOT

Size: Wingspan of 4.3 to 4.7 inches (11 to 12 cm)
Range: Mexico to Argentina
Habitat: Subtropical forests
Diet: Nectar from flowers such as lantanas

CAPE YORK BIRDWING
(ORNITHOPTERA PRIAMUS)

Male Cape York birdwings have bright-green and black forewings. Each hindwing is green with four black dots and black borders. The undersides of the male's wings are green to blue with black veins, black spots, and black edges. The female is larger than the male and has brown wings with white markings on both sides.

HOW TO SPOT

Size: Wingspan of 7 to 8.6 inches (18 to 22 cm)

Range: Australia and New Guinea

Habitat: Tropical rain forests

Diet: Flower nectar

Male

Female

FUN FACT

Cape York birdwings are most active in the early morning and late afternoon. Males can be seen flying high in the rain forest or at rest on the ground.

EASTERN TIGER SWALLOWTAIL
(PAPILIO GLAUCUS)

Male eastern tiger swallowtails have large wings with stripes of bright yellow and black. Females come in two forms. They can have yellow-and-black–striped wings, or they can be all black with a shadow pattern of stripes. In either form, the female has a shiny, blue area on the upper side of each hindwing. Eastern tiger swallowtails can be spotted from May to September in the northern parts of their range, and from February to November in the south.

Male

FUN FACT

The eastern tiger swallowtail is a common garden visitor, especially if the garden has lilac bushes.

HOW TO SPOT

Size: Wingspan of 3.5 to 6.3 inches (8.9 to 16 cm)

Range: Midwestern to eastern North America

Habitat: Gardens, yards, forests, and near streams and rivers

Diet: Nectar from flowers such as lilacs and joe-pye weed

76

FALSE APOLLO *(ARCHON APOLLINUS)*

False Apollos have white, gray, and black markings with two large, black spots on each forewing. Each hindwing is cream colored with a row of black spots. These spots are half circled in red and have blue centers. The undersides of the wings have a similar pattern to the upper sides. Females are larger than males. The false Apollo basks in the sun on rocks, low plants, or the ground. As the butterfly ages, it loses many scales from its forewings. Males tend to lose more scales than females. Older butterflies can have nearly clear forewings.

HOW TO SPOT

Size: Wingspan of 1.8 to 2.1 inches (4.6 to 5.3 cm)
Range: Europe and Asia
Habitat: Woodlands
Diet: Flower nectar

GIANT AFRICAN SWALLOWTAIL
(PAPILIO ANTIMACHUS)

The giant African swallowtail is the largest butterfly in Africa and one of the largest in the world. Its forewings have orange and black markings and brown tips. Its hindwings are orange with black spots and black borders. The undersides of the wings have a similar pattern. Males swoop down from treetops to sip moisture and minerals from mud puddles. The giant African swallowtail has no known predators, except for humans, because it is a very poisonous butterfly.

FUN FACT

Human hunters capture giant African swallowtails and sell them for a large profit. This butterfly is already rare, and both hunting and destruction of the rain forests endanger its survival.

HOW TO SPOT

Size: Wingspan of 6 to 10 inches (15 to 25 cm)

Range: West and central Africa

Habitat: Tropical rain forests

Diet: Flower nectar

THE MYSTERIOUS SWALLOWTAIL

Although the giant African swallowtail was discovered in 1782, little is known about it. Females live high in the forest canopy and are rarely seen.

GOLIATH BIRDWING
(ORNITHOPTERA GOLIATH)

Male goliath birdwings have green forewings with black stripes. Their hindwings are yellow with green veins, green dots, and black edges. Females have dark-brown wings with black, white, and yellow markings. Females tend to be larger than males. Goliath birdwings fly high in the treetops of rain forests. Males chase females before mating begins. The butterfly's numbers have declined due to the destruction of the rain forest and being overcollected by people.

HOW TO SPOT

Size: Wingspan of 8 to 9 inches (20.3 to 22.8 cm)
Range: New Guinea
Habitat: Rain forests
Diet: Flower nectar

Female

Male

LARGE STRIPED SWORDTAIL
(GRAPHIUM ANTHEUS)

Large striped swordtails have black wings with blue markings across their forewings and hindwings. Each hindwing has a long, curved tail. The female tends to be slightly bigger than the male. Sometimes hundreds of males can be seen sipping moisture from a mud puddle together.

HOW TO SPOT

Size: Wingspan of 2.8 to 3.1 inches (7 to 7.9 cm)
Range: Africa
Habitat: Forests
Diet: Flower nectar

MAMBA SWORDTAIL
(GRAPHIUM COLONNA)

Mamba swordtails have black wings with light-blue markings. Each hindwing has a long tail with a white tip. The underside of the mamba's wings is red to brown with light-green markings. This butterfly can be spotted from October to April within its range. It flies slowly and close to the ground in the forest. Males gather and sip moisture and minerals from mud puddles.

FUN FACT

The male mamba sips minerals from wet mud and then passes along the nutrients to the female butterfly during mating.

HOW TO SPOT

Size: Wingspan 2.1 to 2.5 inches (5.3 to 6.3 cm)
Range: Africa
Habitat: Forests
Diet: Flower nectar

MOCKER SWALLOWTAIL
(PAPILIO DARDANUS)

Male mocker swallowtails have pale-yellow forewings with black markings and black tips. The hindwings are also pale yellow with black markings, and they have long tails. The undersides of the male's wings have brown-black spots with black veins. With their yellow wings, the males are easy for predators to spot. In contrast, females have various colorings that mimic different native African butterflies—all of which are either unpleasant to the taste or poisonous. Females also usually lack tails.

HOW TO SPOT

Size: Wingspan of 4 to 4.5 inches (10.2 to 11.4 cm)
Range: Sub-Saharan Africa, including Madagascar
Habitat: Rain forests, cloud forests, botanical gardens, and city parks
Diet: Nectar from flowers such as lantanas

FUN FACT
The mocker swallowtail is extremely alert and active in the early morning, so it's difficult to get close to it at that time.

Male

MANY DIFFERENT LOOKS

A single gene in the female mocker swallowtail acts as a switch that turns on which pattern the female will develop. The female can be black and white, black and orange, white and orange, black and yellow, and many other different combinations.

OLD WORLD SWALLOWTAIL
(PAPILIO MACHAON)

Old World swallowtails have yellow-and-black wings with blue and red markings on the hindwings. Each hindwing has a tail. This butterfly lives only a few weeks. It is a strong flier and can travel long distances. On warm, sunny days, males gather on hilltops and vie for the attention of females flying by. After mating, females lay yellow eggs on host plants such as milk parsley. In the morning and late afternoon, the Old World swallowtail sips nectar from flowers. While sipping, the butterfly flaps its wings constantly to keep its body weight from breaking the delicate flower.

HOW TO SPOT

Size: Wingspan of 2.2 to 3.1 inches (5.6 to 7.9 cm)

Range: Canada, the United States, Europe, Africa, and Asia

Habitat: Grasslands, hilltops, forests, mountains, and tundra in subarctic and arctic areas

Diet: Nectar from flowers such as angelica, knapweeds, marsh thistle, red campion, ragged robin, and valerian

PALAMEDES SWALLOWTAIL
(PAPILIO PALAMEDES)

The Palamedes swallowtail has blackish-brown coloring with two rows of yellow spots on the upper side of its wings. The spots on the inner row blend into a yellow bar on the hindwings. The tails on the hindwings can have yellow stripes down the middle. The undersides of the wings are black with orange, blue, and cream-colored markings. A yellow line crosses the underside of each hindwing. This butterfly has a black body with long, yellow stripes. Spiders prey on these large swallowtails.

HOW TO SPOT

Size: Wingspan of 4.5 to 5.5 inches (11.4 to 14 cm)

Range: Southeastern United States

Habitat: Swamps

Diet: Nectar from flowers such as coastal sweet pepperbush, pickerelweed, and thistles

PIPEVINE SWALLOWTAIL
(BATTUS PHILENOR)

Pipevine swallowtails are medium-sized butterflies with black wings. They have light spots on their forewings and hindwings. The upper side of each hindwing has a blue or blue-green hue, which is brighter on the male than the female. The underside of each hindwing is blue with a row of seven bright-orange spots. There are white spots on the butterfly's abdomen. The pipevine swallowtail flies rapidly, and its wings continue to flutter even when it's perched on a plant.

HOW TO SPOT

Size: Wingspan of 2.8 to 5.1 inches (7 to 13 cm)

Range: Southeastern Canada, the United States, and Mexico

Habitat: Open woods, forest edges, creek banks, and gardens

Diet: Nectar from flowers such as azaleas, lilacs, lantanas, thistles, and petunias

FUN FACT
Pipevine swallowtails taste very bad and can even be poisonous to predators such as birds.

QUEEN ALEXANDRA'S BIRDWING *(ORNITHOPTERA ALEXANDRAE)*

Queen Alexandra's birdwing is the largest butterfly in the world. Males have black wings with green-and-blue streaks and yellow abdomens. Females have brown wings with white markings and yellow abdomens. The female is larger than the male. This butterfly is a strong flier, but it remains close to home. It is found only in the Popondetta area or remote Managalas Plateau in New Guinea. Human activities, especially cutting down rain forests and illegally collecting and trading these butterflies, have had a devastating effect on the Queen Alexandra's birdwing population.

FUN FACT

Predators of the Queen Alexandra's birdwing include small birds and orb-weaving spiders. The butterflies can get caught in the spiders' webs.

HOW TO SPOT

Size: Wingspan of 10.2 to 12 inches (26 to 30 cm)
Range: New Guinea
Habitat: Tropical rain forests
Diet: Nectar from hibiscus flowers

Male

ROTHSCHILD'S BIRDWING
(ORNITHOPTERA ROTHSCHILDI)

Male Rothschild's birdwings tend to be smaller and more colorful than females. Males have brown to black forewings streaked with bands that range in color from cream to green. The hindwings are yellow with black borders, black spots, and green patches. The male's abdomen is yellow. Females have brown forewings with white to gray spots. The female's hindwings have some yellow, white, and brown coloring with dark wing edges. This butterfly is found only at elevations between 5,580 and 8,200 feet (1,700 to 2,500 m) in the remote Arfak Mountains in New Guinea.

Female

Male

HOW TO SPOT

Size: Wingspan of 5.1 to 5.9 inches (13 to 15 cm)
Range: New Guinea
Habitat: Forests
Diet: Flower nectar

RUBY SPOTTED SWALLOWTAIL
(PAPILIO ANCHISIADES)

Ruby spotted swallowtails have mostly black wings with pink, purple, or ruby spots on the hindwings. Females have white patches on their upper forewings. Unlike most swallowtails, these butterflies do not have tails on their hindwings. The ruby spotted swallowtail is active during the day and can be spotted in its range from May to October. Females lay eggs in clusters on the leaves of host plants such as citrus trees. After hatching, the caterpillars lie together on the leaves during the day and eat the leaves at night.

Female

FUN FACT
When threatened, ruby spotted swallowtail caterpillars use their special scent glands to spray chemicals at predators, keeping them away..

HOW TO SPOT

Size: Wingspan of 2.8 to 3.9 inches (7 to 10 cm)

Range: Southern Texas to Argentina

Habitat: Tropical rain forests, citrus groves, and gardens

Diet: Flower nectar

SCARCE SWALLOWTAIL
(IPHICLIDES PODALIRIUS)

Scarce swallowtails have light-yellow wings with vertical, black stripes. Each hindwing has a row of blue spots, an orange-and-blue eyespot, and a long tail. Predators mistake the eyespots and tails for the butterfly's eyes and antennae. This mistake protects the butterfly's real head and gives it more time to escape. The scarce swallowtail can be spotted flying in its range between March and October.

HOW TO SPOT

Size: Wingspan of 2.4 to 3.5 inches (6 to 8.9 cm)

Range: Europe, Turkey, and China

Habitat: Gardens, towns, fields, woodlands, and orchards

Diet: Flower nectar

SPICEBUSH SWALLOWTAIL
(PAPILIO TROILUS)

The spicebush swallowtail's forewings are black with rows of light spots on the wing edges. The hindwings are black with rows of light-green spots. Females have a blue tint while males have a greenish-blue tint. The undersides of the hindwings have rows of bright-orange spots and patches of blue and black. Male spicebush swallowtails get their water from mud puddles. They also draw out minerals from damp soil.

HOW TO SPOT

Size: Wingspan of 3.8 to 4.8 inches (9.7 to 12.2 cm)

Range: Southern Canada and the eastern half of the United States

Habitat: Gardens, forests, fields, roadsides, pine barrens, and swamps

Diet: Nectar from flowers such as azaleas, sweet pepperbush, and jewelweed

Female

WALLACE'S GOLDEN BIRDWING
(ORNITHOPTERA CROESUS)

Male Wallace's golden birdwings have dark-brown coloring and orange bands on their forewings. They also have areas of orange and golden yellow on their hindwings. Underneath, males are black and green. In contrast, females have brown wings with white markings. Females tend to be larger than males. Wallace's golden birdwings can be found visiting flowery shrubs in open areas along paths and waterways.

FUN FACT

Alfred Russel Wallace discovered this butterfly on Bacan, an island in Indonesia, in 1859. He wrote that he was struck by the "beauty and brilliance" of this insect when he first saw it.

HOW TO SPOT

Size: Wingspan of 5.1 to 7.5 inches (13 to 19 cm)
Range: Northern Maluku Islands in Indonesia
Habitat: Wet and swampy areas in forests
Diet: Flower nectar

Male

NO PLACE TO CALL HOME

Forests where Wallace's golden birdwings live have been cut down and cleared by commercial logging operations. Ninety percent of the forests in the northern and central Maluku Islands were subject to logging in the 1980s. As a result, the number of Wallace's golden birdwings declined. Spraying insecticides and overcollecting are also thought to threaten this butterfly.

WESTERN TIGER SWALLOWTAIL *(PAPILIO RUTULUS)*

Western tiger swallowtails have yellow wings with black stripes, edges, and tails. There are small, red spots on the hindwings. The underside of each hindwing has a blue stripe across it. This butterfly can be spotted in its range in midsummer. The male western tiger swallowtail gathers with other swallowtail species to sip moisture from mud puddles. The male also patrols along stream edges and canyons in search of females to mate with. After mating, females can lay up to 100 eggs on different host plants.

HOW TO SPOT

Size: Wingspan of 2.8 to 4 inches (7 to 10.2 cm)

Range: Western United States, from the Rocky Mountains to the coast and north into British Columbia

Habitat: Streams, rivers, canyons, parks, and roadsides

Diet: Nectar from flowers such as zinnias, thistles, milkweeds, and butterfly weed

ZEBRA SWALLOWTAIL
(PROTOGRAPHIUM MARCELLUS)

Zebra swallowtails have white wings with black stripes. The upper side of each hindwing also has a red band and blue spots. Each hindwing has a very long, narrow tail. The undersides of the wings have a similar black-and-white striped pattern, and each hindwing has a red band across it. This butterfly is active in the spring and summer. Zebra swallowtails born in the summer are larger, are darker in color, and have longer tails than those born in the spring.

FUN FACT
Zebra swallowtails that are born in the summer can have tails up to 1 inch (2.5 cm) long.

HOW TO SPOT

Size: Wingspan of 2.5 to 4 inches (6.3 to 10.2 cm)
Range: Eastern United States
Habitat: Waterways, swamps, and marshes
Diet: Flower nectar and mud puddles

BLACK-VEINED WHITE
(APORIA CRATAEGI)

The black-veined white butterfly looks exactly as its name suggests: it has white wings lined with black veins. It can be spotted flying from May to early August in its range. It is a strong flier and can be found at elevations as high as 5,250 feet (1,600 m) above sea level. Males gather and sip moisture from animal droppings, wet soil, and puddles. In Siberia, black-veined whites gather by the thousands to sip moisture from shallow water at the edges of streams. Males and females mate in the late morning on the tops of flowers.

HOW TO SPOT

Size: Wingspan of 2.3 to 2.8 inches (5.8 to 7 cm)

Range: Europe, North Africa, Asia, and Japan

Habitat: Grasslands, woodlands, roadsides, meadows, gardens, and orchards

Diet: Nectar from flowers such as oxeye daisies, thistles, clovers, lavender, and vetch

FUN FACT

Black-veined whites are easily startled. If a male and female are disturbed while mating, the male will carry the female away to a new flower.

BRIMSTONE *(GONEPTERYX RHAMNI)*

Male brimstones have lemon-yellow wings, and females have greenish-white wings. Both the male and female have an orange spot in the middle of each wing. The undersides of the wings are pale green. The brimstone's wings are shaped like leaves, and this gives it excellent camouflage from predators. This butterfly emerges in early spring. It flies until late August or early September, and then it hibernates on ivy plants or underneath bramble leaves. The males and females mate on sunny mornings in early spring.

HOW TO SPOT

Size: Wingspan of 2.4 to 2.9 inches (6 to 7.4 cm)

Range: Europe, North Africa, Asia, and Japan

Habitat: Grasslands, woodlands, farmlands, and coastal areas

Diet: Nectar from a wide variety of flowers, including primroses, bluebells, daisies, buttercups, and thistles

Male

A RESILIENT BUTTERFLY

The brimstone has the longest life span of any butterfly species in Europe. It can live up to 11 months. Most butterflies can live only in certain areas because they need specific plants and weather conditions. The brimstone, however, is a hardy butterfly. It moves around and can be spotted in almost any habitat in its range. It can adapt to different conditions.

CABBAGE WHITE *(PIERIS RAPAE)*

Cabbage whites have white wings with black tips on their forewings. The male has one black spot in the middle of each forewing, and the female has two spots. The cabbage white is one of the earliest butterflies to emerge in the spring. It often flies in swarms. It is a hardy butterfly that can be found in many different habitats. Males patrol for females to mate with near host plants. Females lay eggs on cabbages, radishes, broccoli, and cauliflower plants.

FUN FACT

Unlike most butterflies, the cabbage white thrives in cities, including downtown areas. They have been spotted flying in midtown Manhattan in New York City.

HOW TO SPOT

Size: Wingspan of 1.75 to 2.25 inches (4.4 to 5.7 cm)

Range: North America, Europe, North Africa, Asia, and Australia

Habitat: Gardens, roadsides, fields, and cities

Diet: Nectar from flowers such as dandelions, marigolds, and chrysanthemums

CHECKERED WHITE
(PONTIA PROTODICE)

Male checkered whites have white wings with charcoal markings. Underneath, the male has white coloring. Females have grayish-white wings with darker-gray markings. The undersides of the female's wings are white with yellow markings. The checkered white is active from March through November within its range. It flies quickly and low to the ground. The males sip moisture and get minerals from mud puddles. They often patrol for females on hilltops or other high areas.

HOW TO SPOT

Size: Wingspan of 1.5 to 2.5 inches (3.8 to 6.3 cm)

Range: Southern Canada to northern Mexico

Habitat: Weedy areas, fields, pastures, vacant lots, and roadsides

Diet: Flower nectar from more than 50 different plants

Male

Female

CLOUDED SULPHUR
(COLIAS PHILODICE)

Male clouded sulphurs have bright-yellow wings with black edges. Females have yellow wings, and their black edges have light spots. Both males and females have one black spot on the upper side of each forewing and faint orange spots on the hindwings. The underside of the male's wings is yellow. In the female, the underside is greenish yellow to white. The underside of each hindwing in both males and females has double silver spots circled in pink or brown. This butterfly can be spotted in the northern part of its range from May to October and from March to November in the south.

HOW TO SPOT

Size: Wingspan of 1 to 2 inches (2.5 to 5 cm)

Range: Alaska, Canada, and south to Mexico and Guatemala

Habitat: Fields, lawns, meadows, roadsides, and alfalfa and clover fields

Diet: Nectar from flowers such as clovers, milkweeds, dandelions, and thistles

FUN FACT
Female clouded sulphurs sometimes have white wings instead of yellow.

Female

COMMON GRASS YELLOW
(EUREMA HECABE)

Common grass yellow butterflies have bright-yellow wings with brown edges. Underneath, the wings are a lighter yellow with brown edges. The common grass yellow flies slowly and low to the ground. These butterflies are often seen in grassy areas, but they can be found in many different habitats within their range. The common grass yellow travels long distances and can fly as high as 3,280 feet (1,000 m) above sea level.

HOW TO SPOT

Size: Wingspan of 1.5 inches (3.8 cm)

Range: Africa, Asia, and Australia

Habitat: Gardens, parks, open forests, riverbanks, and roadsides

Diet: Nectar from flowers such as violets and lantanas

GREEN-VEINED WHITE *(PIERIS NAPI)*

Green-veined whites have yellowish-white wings with black on the forewing tips. The male has one black spot in the middle of each forewing, and the female has two. The veins on the undersides of the wings are lined in yellow green. The green-veined white flies early in the morning on cool, cloudy days. In warm, sunny weather it makes short and frequent flights, often stopping to sip nectar from flowers along the way. Males also sip moisture from puddles. The male patrols its area searching for females to mate with. After mating, the female lays eggs on the undersides of the leaves of host plants such as garlic mustard or watercress.

HOW TO SPOT

Size: Wingspan of 1.5 to 2 inches (3.8 to 5 cm)
Range: Europe, Asia, North Africa, and North America
Habitat: Woodlands, riverbanks, and wet meadows
Diet: Nectar from flowers such as dandelions, cuckoo flowers, knapweeds, and thistles

FUN FACT
To find the correct host plants to lay eggs on, females fly to different plants and taste the leaves with sensory structures on their feet.

LITTLE YELLOW *(PYRISITIA LISA)*

As the name suggests, the little yellow butterfly has yellow wings. The wings have black borders and black coloring on the forewing tips. The undersides of the wings are yellow with spots, including two tiny, black dots on each hindwing. Adults have a large, round, reddish-brown spot on the underside of each hindwing, although this mark can be faint or absent in males. Very rarely, a female little yellow can have white wings. Little yellows prefer open, weedy areas.

HOW TO SPOT

Size: Wingspan of 1 to 1.75 inches (2.5 to 4.4 cm)

Range: Midwestern, eastern, and southern United States and south to Costa Rica

Habitat: Roadsides, fields, and prairies

Diet: Nectar from flowers such as asters and goldenrods

NORTHERN CLOUDED YELLOW
(COLIAS HECLA)

Male northern clouded yellows have dark-orange wings with wide, black borders. Females are either orange or white. In both males and females, the undersides of the hindwings are green. This hardy arctic butterfly is active from June to August. It can be spotted flying quickly across the tundra. When it lands, the butterfly blends in well with tundra plants. Females lay eggs on the leaves of host plants, the most common of which is alpine milk vetch.

HOW TO SPOT

Size: Wingspan of 1.4 to 2 inches (3.5 to 5 cm)

Range: Circumpolar north, including Canada, Finland, Denmark, Greenland, Iceland, Norway, Sweden, Russia, and Alaska in the United States

Habitat: Tundras

Diet: Nectar from flowers such as arctic willow, moss campion, and eight-petal mountain avens

THE SHRINKING BUTTERFLY

Research shows that climate change is affecting the northern clouded yellow and other butterflies in Greenland. Rising temperatures have caused snow to melt earlier and summer temperatures to be several degrees warmer. Scientists discovered that the northern clouded yellow's wings are smaller in warmer years. Smaller wings make the butterfly weaker and less able to move around. This change could reduce the northern clouded yellow's ability to reproduce and survive.

ORANGE SULPHUR
(COLIAS EURYTHEME)

Orange sulphur butterflies have yellowish-orange wings with wide borders. Some females have white wings. Both males and females have one or two silver spots circled in pink or black on the underside of each hindwing. Orange sulphurs can also have pink antennae. They fly close to the ground and can be found in open areas from sea level to the mountains.

FUN FACT

Millions of orange sulphurs can swarm alfalfa fields. Their caterpillars are considered pests because they eat alfalfa leaves and damage the plants.

HOW TO SPOT

Size: Wingspan of 2 inches (5 cm)

Range: Southern Canada to central Mexico

Habitat: Agricultural fields, pastures, meadows, and lawns

Diet: Nectar from flowers such as asters, milkweeds, and dandelions

PACIFIC ORANGE-TIP
(ANTHOCHARIS SARA)

Male Pacific orange-tips have white wings and females have white or yellow wings. Each forewing has an orange patch and a black tip. In both the male and female, the underside of each hindwing has a smattering of dark-green markings. The male patrols foothill slopes, valleys, and mountain meadows in search of females to mate with. The female lays eggs on host plants in the mustard family.

FUN FACT

The Pacific orange-tip emerges in the early spring at lower elevations and in late spring to early summer at higher elevations within its range.

HOW TO SPOT

Size: Wingspan of 1.1 to 1.5 inches (2.8 to 3.8 cm)

Range: Alaska and south to Baja California

Habitat: Hills, meadows, orchards, fields, waterways, and canyons

Diet: Nectar from plants such as mustards and thistles

PINE WHITE *(NEOPHASIA MENAPIA)*

Pine whites have white wings with black markings. The undersides of the female's hindwings are rimmed with red. The pine white is active from June to September within its range. It flies slowly, high among the treetops in the forest. The male pine white patrols near host trees, including pines and firs, and searches for females. After mating, females lay eggs on the needles of host trees.

HOW TO SPOT

Size: Wingspan of 1.8 to 2.3 inches (4.6 to 5.8 cm)

Range: Southern British Columbia and the western United States

Habitat: Pine forests

Diet: Flower nectar and moisture from damp sand

SLEEPY ORANGE *(ABAEIS NICIPPE)*

The sleepy orange is an orange butterfly with black borders on the topsides of its wings. There is a small, black mark in the middle of each forewing. Underneath, the butterfly is orangish yellow in the summer and brick red or brown in the winter. The sleepy orange perches with its wings closed. The best time to spot this bright-orange butterfly is when it is flying over open, sunny areas. The sleepy orange is active year-round in the southern part of its range and in mid- to late summer in the northern part.

HOW TO SPOT

Size: Wingspan of 1.5 to 2 inches (3.8 to 5 cm)

Range: United States and Central America

Habitat: Prairies, pine forests, open fields, farmlands, and roadsides

Diet: Nectar from flowers such as tickseed and thistles

106

SOUTHERN DOGFACE
(ZERENE CESONIA)

The southern dogface is a bright-yellow butterfly. On the upper side of each forewing, there is a yellow area with a black spot. The upper sides of the hindwings are yellow. In the summer, the hindwings' undersides are yellow. In the winter, the butterflies have reddish pink coloring along with the yellow. The southern dogface is active year-round in Texas, Florida, and South America.

HOW TO SPOT

Size: Wingspan of 2.1 to 3 inches (5.3 to 7.6 cm)
Range: South America and north to the United States
Habitat: Prairies, pastures, roadsides, fields, and open woodlands
Diet: Nectar from flowers such as alfalfa and verbena

FUN FACT
In the early spring, some southern dogface butterflies travel north as far as Canada. However, they die when freezing temperatures arrive in the fall.

GLOSSARY

bask
To rest and relax in the warm sun.

carrion
The flesh and bones of a dead animal.

chaparrals
Land with thick shrubs and trees.

dung
Animal feces.

host plants
Plants that female butterflies lay eggs on and that caterpillars must feed on to grow into adult butterflies.

mimicry
The close resemblance of one species to another in order to gain an advantage, such as avoiding predators.

oak savannas
Land scattered with oak trees and surrounded by grasses.

patrol
To keep watch over an area by regularly traveling around it.

perch
To rest on something.

pine barrens
Land with sandy soil and pine trees.

scrubs
Land covered with shrubs and small trees.

steppes
Large, flat areas of land that have no trees.

swarm
A very large group of butterflies.

taigas
Subarctic forests with conifer trees that cover vast areas in North America, Europe, and Asia.

woodlands
Land covered with trees.

TO LEARN MORE

FURTHER READINGS

Honovich, Nancy. *1,000 Facts about Insects*. National Geographic, 2018.

Kurlansky, Mark. *Bugs in Danger: Our Vanishing Bees, Butterflies, and Beetles*. Bloomsbury, 2019.

Mooney, Carla. *Insects and Arachnids*. Abdo, 2022.

ONLINE RESOURCES

To learn more about butterflies, please visit **abdobooklinks.com** or scan this QR code. These links are routinely monitored and updated to provide the most current information available.

PHOTO CREDITS

ABDOBOOKS.COM

Published by Abdo Publishing, a division of ABDO, PO Box 398166, Minneapolis, Minnesota 55439. Copyright © 2023 by Abdo Consulting Group, Inc. International copyrights reserved in all countries. No part of this book may be reproduced in any form without written permission from the publisher. Abdo Reference™ is a trademark and logo of Abdo Publishing.

Printed in the United States of America, North Mankato, Minnesota.
052022
092022

THIS BOOK CONTAINS
RECYCLED MATERIALS

Editor: Alyssa Sorenson
Series Designer: Colleen McLaren
Content Consultant: Lynn Kimsey, PhD, professor of entomology, University of California, Davis

Library of Congress Control Number: 2021952335
Publisher's Cataloging-in-Publication Data
Names: Lane, Laura, author.
Title: Butterflies / by Laura Lane
Description: Minneapolis, Minnesota: Abdo Publishing, 2023 | Series: Field guides | Includes online resources and index.
Identifiers: ISBN 9781532198816 (lib. bdg.) | ISBN 9781098272463 (ebook)
Subjects: LCSH: Butterflies--Juvenile literature. | Insects--Juvenile literature. | Insects--Behavior—Juvenile literature. | Animals--Identification--Juvenile literature. | Zoology--Juvenile literature.
Classification: DDC 595.789--dc23